Bible Lessons For Kids

Volume 2

GENESIS 25 – EXODUS 1

Bible Fun Factory

Bible Lessons for Kids

Genesis 25 – Exodus 1

Welcome to this series of original and fantastically fun Bible lessons for students in pre-school through sixth grade. These lessons introduce characters in the book of Genesis and help children make a personal connection by putting the characters problems into a modern day context. The lessons introduce principles students can use every day at school, at home, and in the neighborhood, while growing in Christ.

In this series of five lessons, we focus on the Genesis presentation of Jacob and Joseph, father and son, and how their adventures bring the nation of Israel into being. Students will join Jacob and Esau to learn that **God is always fair**. As Jacob works 14 years to marry Rebekah, we see that sometimes life is not fair, but **God brings justice**. **Courage and persistence** are taught through Jacob wrestling all night with an angel. Jacob has many sons, but his favorite is Joseph. Joseph and his brothers show children how they can **make bad experiences into great experiences**. The final lesson reinforces the lesson on **coura**ge and persistence, showing Moses' mother, who **acted courageously** to save his life.

These lessons bring valuable principles to your students that they will long remember.

Lessons Included:

Lesson 1: Jacob & Esau
Lesson 2: Jacob Works 14 Years
Lesson 3: Jacob Wrestles an Angel
Lesson 4: Joseph & His Brothers
Lesson 5: Moses is Born

A couple notes before you "dig in" to the lesson plans:

We provide more than enough activities to fill a 60 minute class so you can be selective and choose the activities that appeal to you or opt for the activities that match the supplies you have on hand.

The sections written in **BOLD** font type are meant to be a rough "teaching script" for you to use while you are teaching each section. Follow these scripts verbatim or change them to suit your needs!

Contents

Lesson 1

Lesson 2

Lesson 3

Lesson 4

Lesson 5

JACOB AND ESAU

Kids have an internal "justice mechanism" that tells them immediately when something is not fair. As parents, how many times have we heard the lines, "But you let him do it yesterday!" or "You let her stay up late!" or "...not fair, not fair!"

Children want everything in life to be fair, but unfortunately that's not how life works. Looking at the unfair advantage Jacob took of his twin brother Esau gives children a view of reality. The fact that God allowed Jacob's deception can seem confusing, but it is a good opportunity to see **how God is always fair. Things can work out for us even after we've been treated unfairly or have made regrettable mistakes of our own.**

MATERIALS LIST

Lesson

- One giant "stuff bag" for building (should contain household items like small boxes, water bottles, buttons, folded cards, small baskets, caps from used spray containers, clothes pins, etc.) It generally can substitute for building blocks if not enough are available to serve a class project.
- Cardboard box designed as a sky-scraper & hidden away before class

Intro Activity for Younger Children & Older Children

- Slips of paper cut into one-inch squares
- Aluminum foil
- Twist ties or ribbon
- Candy kisses (optional)

Activity, Younger Children

- Dollar Store jewelry boxes or card stock sheets folded in fours to make a skyscraper
- Pre-made example of the skyscraper for them to copy
- Tape
- Glue
- Dried flowers
- Items from "Stuff Box"

Game, Younger Children

- Building blocks

Game, Older Children

- Paper and pencil for each student

Bible Reading / Story:
Genesis 21-33

21 Isaac prayed to the LORD on behalf of his wife, because she was barren. The LORD answered his prayer, and his wife Rebekah became pregnant. 22 The babies jostled each other
within her, and she said, "Why is this happening to me?" So she went to inquire of the LORD.

23 The LORD said to her,

"Two nations are in your womb,
and two peoples from within you will be separated;
one people will be stronger than the other,
and the older will serve the younger."

24 When the time came for her to give birth, there were twin boys in her womb. 25 The first to
come out was red, and his whole body was like a hairy garment; so they named him Esau. 26
After this, his brother came out, with his hand grasping Esau's heel; so he was named Jacob.
Isaac was sixty years old when Rebekah gave birth to them.

27 The boys grew up, and Esau became a skillful hunter, a man of the open country, while
Jacob was a quiet man, staying among the tents. 28 Isaac, who had a taste for wild game,
loved Esau, but Rebekah loved Jacob.

29 Once when Jacob was cooking some stew, Esau came in from the open country, famished.
30 He said to Jacob, "Quick, let me have some of that red stew! I'm famished!" (That is why
he was also called Edom. [g])

31 Jacob replied, "First sell me your birthright."

32 "Look, I am about to die," Esau said. "What good is the birthright to me?"

33 But Jacob said, "Swear to me first." So he swore an oath to him, selling his birthright to Jacob.

34 Then Jacob gave Esau some bread and some lentil stew. He ate and drank, and then got up and left.

So Esau despised his birthright.

Genesis 27: Jacob Gets Isaac's Blessing

1 When Isaac was old and his eyes were so weak that he could no longer see, he called for Esau his older son and said to him, "My son."

"Here I am," he answered.

2 Isaac said, "I am now an old man and don't know the day of my death. 3 Now then, get your
weapons—your quiver and bow—and go out to the open country to hunt some wild game for
me. 4 Prepare me the kind of tasty food I like and bring it to me to eat, so that I may give you
my blessing before I die."

5 Now Rebekah was listening as Isaac spoke to his son Esau. When Esau left for the open country to hunt game and bring it back, 6 Rebekah said to her son Jacob, "Look, I overheard your
father say to your brother Esau, 7 'Bring me some game and prepare me some tasty food to
eat, so that I may give you my blessing in the presence of the LORD before I die.' 8 Now, my
son, listen carefully and do what I tell you: 9 Go out to the flock and bring me two choice young
goats, so I can prepare some tasty food for your father, just the way he likes it. 10 Then take it
to your father to eat, so that he may give you his blessing before he dies."

11 Jacob said to Rebekah his mother, "But my brother Esau is a hairy man, and I'm a man with
smooth skin. 12 What if my father touches me? I would appear to be tricking him and would
bring down a curse on myself rather than a blessing."

13 His mother said to him, "My son, let the curse fall on me. Just do what I say; go and get
them for me."

14 So he went and got them and brought them to his mother, and she prepared some tasty
food, just the way his father liked it. 15 Then Rebekah took the best clothes of Esau her older
son, which she had in the house, and put them on her younger son Jacob. 16 She also covered
his hands and the smooth part of his neck with the goatskins. 17 Then she handed to her son
Jacob the tasty food and the bread she had made.

18 He went to his father and said, "My father."

"Yes, my son," he answered. "Who is it?"

19 Jacob said to his father, "I am Esau your firstborn. I have done as you told me. Please sit up
and eat some of my game so that you may give me your blessing."

20 Isaac asked his son, "How did you find it so quickly, my son?"

"The LORD your God gave me success," he replied.

21 Then Isaac said to Jacob, "Come near so I can touch you, my son, to know whether you
really are my son Esau or not."

22 Jacob went close to his father Isaac, who touched him and said, "The voice is the voice of
Jacob, but the hands are the hands of Esau." 23 He did not recognize him, for his hands were

hairy like those of his brother Esau; so he blessed him. 24 "Are you really my son Esau?" he
asked.

"I am," he replied.

25 Then he said, "My son, bring me some of your game to eat, so that I may give you my blessing."

Jacob brought it to him and he ate; and he brought some wine and he drank. 26 Then
his father Isaac said to him, "Come here, my son, and kiss me."

27 So he went to him and kissed him. When Isaac caught the smell of his clothes, he blessed him and said,

"Ah, the smell of my son
is like the smell of a field
that the LORD has blessed.

28 May God give you of heaven's dew
and of earth's richness—
an abundance of grain and new wine.

29 May nations serve you
and peoples bow down to you.
Be lord over your brothers,
and may the sons of your mother bow down to you.
May those who curse you be cursed
and those who bless you be blessed."

30 After Isaac finished blessing him and Jacob had scarcely left his father's presence, his
brother Esau came in from hunting. 31 He too prepared some tasty food and brought it to his
father. Then he said to him, "My father, sit up and eat some of my game, so that you may give
me your blessing."

32 His father Isaac asked him, "Who are you?"

"I am your son," he answered, "your firstborn, Esau."

33 Isaac trembled violently and said, "Who was it, then, that hunted game and brought it to me? I ate it just before you came and I blessed him—and indeed he will be blessed!"

34 When Esau heard his father's words, he burst out with a loud and bitter cry and said to his father, "Bless me—me too, my father!"

35 But he said, "Your brother came deceitfully and took your blessing."

36 Esau said, "Isn't he rightly named Jacob? He has deceived me these two times: He took my birthright, and now he's taken my blessing!" Then he asked, "Haven't you reserved any blessing for me?"

37 Isaac answered Esau, "I have made him lord over you and have made all his relatives his servants…

Jacob Flees to Laban

41 Esau held a grudge against Jacob because of the blessing his father had given him. He said to himself, "The days of mourning for my father are near; then I will kill my brother Jacob."

42 When Rebekah was told what her older son Esau had said, she sent for her younger son
Jacob and said to him, "Your brother Esau is consoling himself with the thought of killing you.
43 Now then, my son, do what I say: Flee at once to my brother Laban in Haran.

Genesis 33: Jacob Meets Esau

1 Jacob looked up and there was Esau, coming with his four hundred men; so he divided the
children among Leah, Rachel and the two maidservants. 2 He put the maidservants and their
children in front, Leah and her children next, and Rachel and Joseph in the rear. 3 He himself
went on ahead and bowed down to the ground seven times as he approached his brother.

4 But Esau ran to meet Jacob and embraced him; he threw his arms around his neck and kissed him. And they wept.

8 Esau asked, "What do you mean by all these droves [livestock and gifts that Jacob had sent out to him] I met?"

"To find favor in your eyes, my lord," he said.

9 But Esau said, "I already have plenty, my brother. Keep what you have for yourself."

Lesson (Teacher Words In Bold): God Is Always Fair

Today we're going to build skyscrapers. Dump a mountain of "stuff" onto the floor or a table. A "stuff" bag is always fun. It can contain all sorts of things for building and imagining. (See Materials List)

Children should use their imaginations to build their own "skyscrapers."

To minimize arguments, only one piece of the "stuff" can be taken at a time to build each skyscraper. Students will become intent on building quickly so they can grab the next piece of "stuff."

Walk past a kid and accidentally knock down his skyscraper.

Oops. I'm terribly sorry. It looks like we've had an accident. How does it feel to have your skyscraper knocked down?

Child may allude to feeling annoyed or may even say, "Not fair!"

But it was an accident. Do you forgive me? How about if I help you build it again?

Help the child build it again.

Look for a nice, firm, supportive piece of stuff in another child's skyscraper.

Wow, look at that piece! That would surely help me and (child whom you are helping) build ours better.

Take the piece of stuff and give it to the child whom you are helping, even if it knocks down the other child's skyscraper.

I'm sorry if I ruined your skyscraper, but we really needed that piece to build ours. You don't mind, do you?

The child should make statements to the contrary.

Does that feel unfair to you? Well, who says everything has to be fair?

To the class: **Has anything ever happened to you that was unfair? Tell us about it**.

Encourage the children to speak up. Everyone should have a story about something unfair happening to them.

Do you think that your parents are ever unfair?

Variations of: yes.

So, why do you still love them?

Variations of: nobody's perfect.

Do you think Sunday school teachers can be unfair? (While asking, take a piece off somebody's sky scraper and add it to a different child's sky scraper.)

But you still come to Sunday school. Why?

Variations of: because we overlook the bad to have the fun.

Do you know that I love you?

Variations of: yes.

The point is that everyone on earth can be unfair sometimes. Jacob stole Esau's birthright, and his mom helped him. Was that fair?

Variations of: no.

And yet, God allowed the birthright to stay with Jacob. God didn't come along and give the birthright back to Esau.

Here is a tough question. Is God ever unfair?

Let the students discuss this.

God is always fair. Sometimes God allows other people to be unfair, but He does not act unfairly Himself. Let's look at Esau. He was treated unfairly, but God gave him so much stuff that when Jacob came to meet him, offering him sheep and cows and livestock, Esau said, "Keep your stuff. I have more than enough of my own."

Sometimes God allows unfairness for a while, but He likes to make it up to us.

Go to the hiding place and bring out the cardboard box you made before class to look like a skyscraper.

Put the cardboard skyscraper in front of the child from whose skyscraper you stole and did not return anything.

God is always fair. Sometimes His story isn't over yet.

Intro Activity, Younger & Older Children:
Candy Kisses Game

Cut up slips of paper into one-inch squares. Put one word on each slip: God. is. always. fair. Sometimes. His. story. isn't. over. yet.

Fold the slips or crinkle them into tiny balls and wrap them in aluminum foil to look like candy kisses. Hide them around the room.

Tell the children as they arrive that there are 10 treasures hidden around the room. They can open them as they find them.

Once they are all opened, the jumbled words will seem confusing.

Once all of the students have arrived, put all ten words on a table.

Sometimes it's hard to see God's will. Sometimes things look unfair. Sometimes only God knows the order of things.

Put all the words in order.

Sometimes we have to wait and be patient and thoughtful to make sense of the things God is doing in our lives.

Suggestion: Have one real candy kiss for everyone.

Activity, Younger Children:
Building Skyscrapers with Cardstock

Build skyscrapers using cardstock folded in fours so that it will wrap around with four sides. Show students an example. Show them how you will tape the ends together securely and evenly so that the tube will stand after they are finished drawing on windows and doors.

Using things from the "stuff" box such as buttons and flowers and little scraps of cloth, tell the children to create their own skyscraper.

Show them how to draw windows before adding buttons (doorways, roofing pieces) and dried flowers for gardens at the bottom.

Encourage them to use their imaginations, using whatever small household things are in the stuff box.

Sometimes things look unfair. Sometimes it appears that God is being unfair, but He's not. If God allowed an unfair person to steal from you—even if it was your house—don't despair. It might be that later He'll give you something much bigger.

Activity, Older Children: Discussion

As children have a strong sense of justice, have them each share a time when they were treated unfairly.

Everyone should be able to think of one. Discuss how they reacted, then discuss how they might have handled it better.

Let's look at Esau. In a family as wealthy as Isaac's, a birthright is like a chance to be king. Let's look at Christ and what he said in Matthew 5:39: "But I tell you, Do not resist an evil person. If someone strikes you on the right cheek, turn to him the other also."

Now, ask them tougher questions. Ask about a time when they did something that was unfair to someone else. Ask each student to remember why he did it. If they have trouble being honest, present a very honest example from your own life.

Some people falsely believe that if God were really fair, He would wipe all unfairness off the face of the earth. But then, what would happen to us?

(In answer to the supposition that God should be able to remove unfairness and leave the rest of our character alone: We are people; we're not robots. We wouldn't want God to simply 're-program' us. We would miss an opportunity to learn something, and God wants us to grow.)

As for people who've been unfair to you, think of some ways God may have made it up to you. What did you learn from that experience?

(Examples: Made us better, stronger, more patient people…)

And there's a great expression: "It ain't over 'til it's over." If you think you were treated unfairly and God hasn't made it up to you yet, keep watching.

Game, Younger Children: The Skyscraper Game

Get out actual building blocks this time and tell the children they're going to build a sky-scraper again, this time with blocks.

Have each child take turns adding two blocks. Rotate until everyone has taken three or four turns.

If someone accidentally topples the skyscraper, have the others say, "That's all right! You're still on my team!"

That child gets another turn, even if it's to start over again.

Once a skyscraper has been erected, talk about teamwork:

Look at the beautiful building we can make if we all work together! We may argue a lot with our sisters and brothers, but we can't forget that they're on our team. Jacob and Esau were brothers. They both ended up with a lot of tall stuff in their lives, but they were so busy being mad at each other that they never learned to work as a team.

How much greater might they have been had they decided to work together?

Let's always remember to forgive our sisters and brothers and friends. Let's remember that they're always on our team. We have a much better chance if we all build something together.

Game, Older Children: Anagram

On the chalkboard, write the phrase "God is always fair."

Then instruct students to use the anagram to create as many words (three letters or more) as possible. To make this activity more challenging, increase the three letter rule to four letters or more.

Once students use the designated amount of time, ask students, **Do you think that there are more words that our class hasn't thought of?** Once students say yes, ask, **Why do you think that?**

Answer: God is always fair. Sometimes his story isn't over yet.

Closing Prayer

Dear Lord, Help us to remember this week to always be fair, even if others are not being fair to us. Even though we might not always understand at the time, help us to believe that You are the one who makes everything fair in the end.

Amen.

JACOB WORKS 14 YEARS

In the previous lesson, you discussed how children do not like when it appears they've been treated unfairly. Their internal sense of justice works quite well, and at the same time, it is important to reinforce to them that things do not always go the way we want them to. Oldest siblings are often held more responsible for what may be the younger child's fault. **In a world that is not always fair, the best answer is to wait on God's justice. We get what we're after when it's a good thing, and when we are patient.**

MATERIALS LIST

Lesson

- Nothing required

Intro Activity for Younger Children

- Regular scrub bucket or box about the same size
- One blank sheet of paper

Intro Activity for Older Children

- One sheet of paper for each student

Activity, Younger Children

- Bucket and sheet of paper used in Intro Activity

Activity, Older Children

- Paper airplanes used in Intro Activity
- Hula-hoop (or if you don't have one, use a hanger with the center pulled down so it makes a diamond or "hoop").

Game, Younger Children

- Blindfold
- Toys from the classroom, one for each child

Game, Older Children

- Large cardboard box, at least 24 inches square
- Thirty blocks that are rectangular or triangular
- One complete square block, or one regular block with masking tape around it

BIBLE READING / STORY:
GENESIS 29:14-27

After Jacob had stayed with him for a whole month, 15 Laban said to him, "Just because you
are a relative of mine, should you work for me for nothing? Tell me what your wages should
be."

16 Now Laban had two daughters; the name of the older was Leah, and the name of the
younger was Rachel. 17 Leah had delicate features, but Rachel was lovely in form, and beautiful. 18 Jacob was in love with Rachel and said, "I'll work for you seven years in return for your
younger daughter Rachel."

19 Laban said, "It's better that I give her to you than to some other man. Stay here with me." 20
So Jacob served seven years to get Rachel, but they seemed like only a few days to him because of his love for her.

21 Then Jacob said to Laban, "Give me my wife. My time is completed, and I want to lie with
her."

22 So Laban brought together all the people of the place and gave a feast. 23 But when evening
came, he took his daughter Leah and gave her to Jacob, and Jacob lay with her. 24 And Laban
gave his servant girl Zilpah to his daughter as her maidservant.

25 When morning came, there was Leah! So Jacob said to Laban, "What is this you have done
to me? I served you for Rachel, didn't I? Why have you deceived me?"

26 Laban replied, "It is not our custom here to give the younger daughter in marriage before
the older one. 27 Finish this daughter's bridal week; then we will give you the younger one also,
in return for another seven years of work."

28 And Jacob did so. He finished the week with Leah, and then Laban gave him his daughter
Rachel to be his wife. 29 Laban gave his servant girl Bilhah to his daughter Rachel as her maidservant. 30 Jacob lay with Rachel also, and he loved Rachel more than Leah. And he worked
for Laban another seven years.

Lesson (Teacher Words In Bold): Jacob Learns About God's Honesty

Through Jacob and Esau, we saw how life is not always fair. This week, it was Jacob who was put in the unfair position. Jacob worked for seven years before he could marry the woman he loved... that is a long time. And then, who does he end up with? Her sister, whom he did not love. To get the girl he loved, he had to work another seven years.

Can you think of a time when you were treated unfairly? Maybe when you were blamed for something you didn't do? Let the children answer.

Some prompts:

- Parents punished you when a sister or brother started a fight.
- Teacher blamed you for a class upset without hearing your side.

These are very frustrating examples. God has an answer on how to handle times like these. Like most things of God—it's simple, but it's not always easy.

Have your students form a circle around one person, who is considered "in the trap." If you don't have an even total number of students, have your assistant join in.

Sometimes we find ourselves in a "sticky mess," as they say. That means a problem starts coming upon us, sort of like Jacob's problem.

Instruct all students to take hold out their left hands and take the left hand of someone else. It cannot be the person standing next to them. It can be the person in the trap. It can be someone across the trap from them. Then, have them join right hands using the same principle, only they may not join their right hands with those whom their left hands are joined. They cannot let go of the other person's left hand. If they do, try to join the hands again or find another hand, including the person in the trap until everyone is joined together without using the person next to them.

Sometimes, we find the problem is even worse than we initially thought.

Sometimes we feel really trapped. Sometimes we *are* really trapped. One way of finding yourself in a trap is having been lied to, like Jacob was. Have you ever had a friend promise you something great and not come through?

Ask the student in the trap to try to get out to you, standing several feet on the outside without breaking the trap or anyone else moving their feet.

Sometimes when we really feel trapped; our first instinct is to try to get out of it ourselves, without God's help. It's very hard and sometimes impossible to get out of an unfair situation. But God sees all, and God is good. Often, when we're not expecting it, He *will* bring justice for us if we're *patient*.

Instruct the student in the trap to let go of his human friend and join his left hand with your hand. Then he should let of his other human friend and join his right hand with your hand. Remove him from the circle keeping both his hands in yours.

Isaiah 40:31 says, "They that wait on the Lord will renew their strength. They will mount up with wings like eagles."

Let's learn to wait on God to make things fair.

Intro Activity, Younger Children: Paper-in-the-Bucket Game

Today we're going to talk about fairness again and how sometimes life isn't fair. Here's a game to play to demonstrate.

Have a child stand over a bucket holding a flat sheet of 8.5 x 11 paper. Tell her to let go of the paper and see if she can get it in the bucket without folding it or crunching it up.

Keep trying to get the paper in the bucket. Sometimes it will go in and sometimes it won't. This goes to show how we can't always control what happens. But we'll see in the lesson how God can help us with life's drifting events.

Intro Activity, Older Children: Paper Airplane Trips

Sometimes life is not fair. It seems like somebody gets something better than we do, even if it's a thing we really wanted, and even if it seems like they don't deserve it. It's sort of like paper airplanes...

Have arriving students make a paper airplane out of a sheet of paper. Easy instructions are as follows if they don't know how to do this. Have each student:

Lay the sheet in front of himself length-wise.

Fold the two top corners down, so they meet in the middle and press them flat.

Fold each folded portion toward the center once again, so the folds meet in the middle again and press them flat.

Fold the edges of the paper backwards to make wings.

Have them fly their airplanes into a corner, but not at each other!

The airplanes are all made the same way, but they are all slightly different. Some of you are better at folding. Some of you have stronger arms to fly things. You don't know, when you're flying alone, "flying without God," how close to your targets you'll land, do you?

Activity, Younger Children: Ball in the Bucket Game

We saw earlier today how one very light piece of paper is hard to aim. It's a little like us when we try to do things without God. We flit all about and don't necessarily end up with what we want. When we ball the paper up (ball the paper used in the Intro Activity into a hard ball) **it is easier to direct, isn't it?**

We Christians are a little like this paper ball. After asking God to be with us, he comes into our lives and begins to "reshape" our spirits. We become easier for him to direct. Throw the paper into the bucket. **Let's remember to ask God to keep reshaping our spirits, so that when it's time to get into heaven someday, he can say we are slam-dunks!**

Have students stand behind maybe six feet from the bucket. They get three tries to get the ball in the bucket.

If a student can't hit the bucket: **God understands that we're all different, and he wants to help us in whatever way we need him.**

Move the bucket closer so the child can make the basket.

Activity, Older Children: Airplane through the Hoop Game

We saw earlier today how airplanes don't always aim very well. It's a little like us when we try to do things without God. We flit all about and don't necessarily end up where we want. One thing the Lord does is give us a direction. If we can see His will for us, it gives us something to "aim for." Let's practice.

Use either a hula hoop or a hanger bent so that it makes a large diamond. Give the children back their paper airplanes. Standing six feet away, see if the children can aim their airplanes and get them through the hoop. Each child gets three tries. Keep telling them they are close and to try a little harder if they miss.

For those who can't make it through the hoop from this distance: **God knows we're all individuals, and he wants to help us each in the individual ways that we need.**

Bring the hoop closer to that child as close as he or she needs to get the airplane through. Move the hoop back if a child gets his through repeatedly.

Game, Younger Children: Finding God's Will Game

Jacob worked for fourteen years to earn the right from his Uncle to marry Rebekah. Sometimes God's way is not easy, but it always brings the best rewards. Sometimes it feels like we're not seeing where we're going, but the small voice of God is always present to show the way.

Blindfold one child. Have the other children form a big circle. Give one child a toy from the room. Tell the blindfolded child what it is and to find which child is holding it.

The blindfolded child should make her way to each child and feel their arms to see if they're holding anything. Students can direct her only by saying "backward!" or "forward!" or "side!" They should all shout at once. It should get very confusing. Stand behind the child holding the toy and in a still, small voice, say:

Come to me... Come to me. Or **come this way... come this way...** and let her follow your voice to where you want her to be.

Repeat with blindfolding each child and using a different toy each time. When they are finished:

Finding the toy blindfolded is a little like finding God's will in life. God's will is definitely there, and we have the Holy Spirit and angels to help us find it. Just like you all found the toy, you can all find God's will!

Game, Older Children: The Dark Box

Bring out a box. You should have about 30 standard kids' building blocks in it, and only one square block (the kind with the alphabet letters on it). It's best if the box has a lid, but a towel will work.

We've talked about listening to God's voice, and how it's not always easy to find the way. But there's joy at the other end—once we find God's will and follow it. Let's practice using this box.

Let the children look in the box, seeing the standard blocks and the one square alphabet block. Shake the box before each child takes his turn. Have children take turns sticking one hand in. Tell them **"God's will" is like the square block. We need to find it while there are so many things to distract us. Find the square block and you've found God's will!**

Repeat until each child has found the square block.

(Note: If you don't have a square block, put a piece of masking tape or electrical tape around one block. Show them the block before the game starts, and tell them that's 'God's Will'.)

Closing Prayer

Father, Thank you for always providing a light to show us the way. Give us hope every day to follow You and not listen to the sounds of the world.

Amen.

JACOB WRESTLES AN ANGEL

Some previous lessons have touched upon patience and its importance in following God's plans. The story of Jacob wrestling all night with the angels is a good story to show another great Christian virtue in action - persistence. **Sometimes God wants us to wait patiently for him,** as Jacob waited the seven years to marry Rachel, **and sometimes God wants us to be persistent and proceed courageously. Those who persist in the right things get blessed!**

MATERIALS LIST

Lesson

In church refrigerator before the start of class place:

- Pint of whipping cream
- Metal mixing bowl
- Metal whisk

Also needed:

- Three tablespoons of sugar
- Pie or pudding cups, enough for each child to have a serving
- Plastic spoons and plates

Intro Activity, Younger Children

- No materials needed

Intro Activity, Older Children

- One list of the following book titles: Genesis, Exodus, Judges, Joshua, Samuel, Psalms

Activity, Younger Children

- Light colored construction paper, one sheet for each child
- Large buttons (light color if possible), one for each child
- Bright and dark colored marker pens

- Glue sticks
- One sheet yellow construction paper with moons cut out, one moon for each child
- Four sheets of brightly colored tissue paper for cutting out angel wings, one set of wings for each child
- Stapler
- Scotch tape
- Glitter
- Aluminum foil
- Scissors

Activity, Older Children

- Several discarded graphic novels, which children can use to refer to or to cut out various graphics that they like
- Scissors
- Glue sticks
- Pencils
- White sheets of drawing paper, one for each child

Game, Younger and Older Children

- Aluminum foil, enough to crinkle into two balls the size of a baseball
- Four large slotted spoons
- Prizes for all (snack)

Bible Reading / Story:
Genesis 32

Jacob worked twenty years for Lebon, 14 years to have Leah and Rachel for wives and six years to support them. Everything Jacob touched, God blessed, but Lebon kept cheating him, and in the middle of the night, he took his wives and flocks and all his belongings and started out for the homeland of his father Isaac.

Genesis 32: Jacob Wrestles With God

22 That night Jacob got up and took his two wives, his two maidservants and his eleven sons
and crossed the ford of the Jabbok. 23 After he had sent them across the stream, he sent over
all his possessions. 24 So Jacob was left alone, and a man (angel) wrestled with him till daybreak. 25 When the man saw that he could not overpower him, he touched the socket of
Jacob's hip so that his hip was wrenched as he wrestled with the man. 26 Then the man said,
"Let me go, for it is daybreak."

But Jacob replied, "I will not let you go unless you bless me."

27 The man asked him, "What is your name?"

"Jacob," he answered.

28 Then the man said, "Your name will no longer be Jacob, but Israel, because you have struggled with God and with men and have overcome."

29 Jacob said, "Please tell me your name."

But he replied, "Why do you ask my name?" Then he blessed him there.

30 So Jacob called the place Peniel, saying, "It is because I saw God face to face, and yet my life was spared."

31 The sun rose above him as he passed Peniel, and he was limping because of his hip. 32 Therefore to this day the Israelites do not eat the tendon attached to the socket of the hip, because
the socket of Jacob's hip was touched near the tendon.

LESSON (TEACHER WORDS IN BOLD): WITH PERSISTENCE, JACOB BECOMES "ISRAEL"

For this exercise, you'll need the kids to make a road trip to the church kitchen. Before class starts place a pint of heavy cream, a metal bowl and a whisk in the refrigerator.

"If you don't give up on the little things, you won't give up on the big things."

That is a famous saying and one we should all put in our hearts. Persistence means to NEVER GIVE UP. Every day we have to persist in the little things.

Let's practice. First, we're going to take a trip together to the church kitchen and see what the Lord has in store for us. To get there, we're going to practice patience, and its first cousin, persistence.

Have the children line up. Tell them they're going to walk by putting the heel of one foot to the toe of their other foot to take one step. Then they repeat with the other foot, sort of as if they're walking on a board and trying to keep their balance. The important thing is that their heel should meet their toe without any spaces with each foot and each step. Depending on how far the kitchen is (and how big their feet are), try to keep them walking like that for three minutes. They may then "rest," which is walk normally, to complete the rest of the trip.

On the way, have them recite this poem (though softly so as not to disturb other Sunday school classes):

Jacob fought the angel
All through the night.
He huffed and he puffed
And he fought with might.
He got very tired
But he wouldn't be through.
Jacob was persistent
In Genesis 32.

It will make the walk to a little quicker.

When you get to the kitchen, have the children get the materials (pint, metal bowl, and whisk) out of the refrigerator.

Now we're going to practice patience and persistence again, only this time in another way. This time, we're going to walk backwards...slowly, so we don't bang into anything.

Make certain they understand not to skip or run backwards—*one step at a time.*

When Jacob was in love with Rachel, he took one step at a time. He was patient and persistent for seven years. He didn't always know where he was going, just as we don't. He had to feel for God's way. Let's practice, and see how far we can get if we go slowly and try not to bang into each other.

Repeat the rhyme *slowly and soothingly,* which will keep their energy manageable.

Once back in the classroom, pour the heavy cream into the cold metal dish. Add three tablespoons of sugar.

If we're very persistent in our whisking, we can turn this cream into whipped cream, but it takes a lot of beating to make whipped cream by hand. Who wants to try? And while we're working on that, we'll talk more about persistence.

Demonstrate how hard and fast you actually have to whisk to make whipped cream. Then let the children take turns whisking; have an assistant hold the bowl so nobody spills it over. It takes about seven minutes to whip cream by hand (and it must be cold first!). Hence, while kids take turn whisking, ask questions about how they can apply persistence to their lives. Prompts:

Who is trying to improve on a sport?

Which sports?

What do you have to do to improve?

Have you asked God to be part of that sport with you?

Let's ask him now: Say a prayer so that the children will realize that God wants to be part of everything and he will teach them persistence.

Who is trying to improve in school?

What subjects?

What specifically do you have to do to improve?

Have you asked God to be part of your studies with you?

Let's ask him now: Say a prayer so that the children will realize that God wants to be part of everything and he will teach them persistence.

Who is trying to get along better with a sister, brother or friend?

What can you do so that this person might enjoy spending more time with you?

Have you asked God to help build that relationship?

Let's ask him now: Say a prayer so that the children will realize that God wants to be part of that relationship too, and he will teach them patience and persistence.

By this point, if everyone has whisked hard, you ought to have whipped cream.

Look what we did with our persistence... Ta da!! Whipped cream!

Top either a pie or pudding cups with the whipped cream and let everyone enjoy.

Intro Activity, Younger Children: Persistence Mini-Contests

Today, we're going to learn how Jacob wrestled a blessing away from one of God's angels. He had to show "persistence." To start, we're going to show some persistence with a game.

Have contests to see who can do things the longest like stand on one foot, holding the other foot in one hand without touching anything; holding their breath; go the farthest through the letters by saying the alphabet backwards, etc.

Intro Activity, Older Children: Spelling Game

Today, we're going to learn about Jacob having persistence against an angel. He wrestled the angel all night so the angel would bless him. We're going to show a different sort of persistence in the following difficult game.

Have a list of the books of the Bible that are easier to spell. Spell it for the students until they have them memorized, then ask them to spell the books backwards, without looking or writing them down:

Genesis	Judges	Samuel
Exodus	Joshua	Psalms

Play with one student until others arrive, then give the list to the student who totally hates to spell and let him/her be the referee by checking the words.

Activity, Younger Children:
Jacob Fights the Angel Picture

Have the children draw a picture of Jacob fighting the angel, using some cut out shapes you made from the Materials List. They can use glue stick when appropriate:

- Have the moon on one side of the picture and the sun on the other (to show "all night"). The sun can be a button put on with glue stick, with crayon rays coming out of it. The moon can be cutouts from the yellow construction paper.
- The angel's wings can be four sheets of tissue paper put together and cut into wing shapes, one under the other, so that each child gets four wings. Each child should lay the wings on their angel's back. Staple it down in the very center, and when they pull up on the tissue paper, it will make wings. (Tape down staples after for younger children!)
- Put glitter on Jacob's leg and arm muscles and on his hip where the angel struck him.
- Make little crowns out of aluminum foil (cut in a 1-inch square, with three jagged points at the top). The angel can be handing the crown to Joseph, or it can be off to the side on a rock.
- Have everyone write at the top **JACOB WRESTLES THE ANGEL: GENESIS 32**.

Activity, Older Children:
Graphic Novel: Jacob and the Angel

Have two or three discarded graphic novels on the art table for children to copy. (Other exercises call for these, so you can keep these and use them again.)

The story goes that Jacob persisted against the angel all night because he wanted to be blessed. You can draw that, or you can draw some situation of your own where you need to show a lot of persistence. The game is to make a graphic novel page out of the situation.

Using sharp pencils, they can copy the styles of the graphic novels available, or they can cut out the artists' speech bubbles or artwork to add to their own. They should each have somewhere on the page… Persistence Reigns.

Game, Younger and Older Children:
Catching With Spoons Game

Sometimes it's not easy to persist. Sometimes we want to give up on something hard, but the person who persists gets the prize!

Have children form two relay teams at one end of the room. If there is an odd number, the first child on the team with less people can go twice. Give the first two children on each team a large tablespoon or slotted spoon (that's four big spoons in all). Put a piece of aluminum foil, rolled up like a baseball into one of the spoons on each time (that's two aluminum baseballs).

Show the players how to toss the "ball" back and forth to each other, catching it on the spoon. Then, they have to start moving slowly to the other end of the room while tossing back and forth.

One catch without dropping the ball earns one step forward by both teammates. A dropped ball means they have to stay where they are and try again, until a caught ball earns them a step forward.

Once a team reaches the far wall, they can run back with the spoons and ball and deliver to the next set of players.

Whichever team finishes first wins.

Ask, **who should get the prize?** They should answer that the winning team should. However remind them:

God is not as interested in how fast or how slow we are. He is interested in those who *show* persistence. Therefore, everyone gets a prize.

Pass out cookies, licorice sticks, or other available prizes.

Closing Prayer

Father, Show us how You are always with us, even when situations require persistence. Give us Your strength, and keep reminding us of how great the rewards are when we stick with something difficult.

Amen.

JOSEPH AND HIS BROTHERS

God Turns Bad Things into Good Things

All children can relate to good and bad times within their family. There may be sibling rivalry or lying, or worse situations such as divorce.

In seeing one of the worst family disasters in human history, children will be able to put their own family's issues into perspective. Jealousy, sibling rivalry, and covering up deception could have hurt Joseph irreparably, but with God's presence, he became introspective, selfless and a great leader. **God turns bad things into good things. That is always a valuable lesson.**

MATERIALS LIST

Lesson

- 1 whole lemon
- 2 pieces of plastic wrap
- 1 twist tie
- 1 Sharpie
- 4 lemons cut in quarters
- 1 cup sugar
- Pitcher
- Water
- Wooden or plastic serving spoon to stir lemonade

Intro Activity for Younger Children

- Construction Paper
- Crayons

Intro Activity for Older Children

- Paper and pencils

Activity, Younger Children

- Old neckties or pieces of string for tying hands together
- Animal Crackers
- Wet paper towel

Activity, Older Children

- Costumes (optional)

Game, Younger Children

- Old neckties or pieces of string for tying legs together (use from Activity)

Game, Older Children

- Toilet paper sheets torn into squares

Bible Reading / Story: Genesis 37-43

Joseph's Dreams

2a Joseph, a young man of seventeen, was tending the flocks with his brothers.

3 Now Israel [Jacob] loved Joseph more than any of his other sons, because he had been born to him in his old age; and he made a richly ornamented robe for him. 4 When his brothers saw that their father loved him more than any of them, they hated him and could not speak a kind word to him.

5 Joseph had a dream, and when he told it to his brothers, they hated him all the more. 6 He said to them, "Listen to this dream I had: 7 We were binding sheaves of grain out in the field when suddenly my sheaf rose and stood upright, while your sheaves gathered around mine and bowed down to it."

8 His brothers said to him, "Do you intend to reign over us? Will you actually rule us?" And they hated him all the more because of his dream and what he had said.

9 Then he had another dream, and he told it to his brothers. "Listen," he said, "I had another dream, and this time the sun and moon and eleven stars were bowing down to me."

10 When he told his father as well as his brothers, his father rebuked him and said, "What is this dream you had? Will your mother and I and your brothers actually come and bow down to the ground before you?" 11 His brothers were jealous of him, but his father kept the matter in mind.

Joseph Sold by His Brothers

Joseph went after his brothers and found them near Dothan. 18 But they saw him in the distance, and before he reached them, they plotted to kill him.

19 "Here comes that dreamer!" they said to each other. 20 "Come now, let's kill him and throw him into one of these cisterns and say that a ferocious animal devoured him. Then we'll see what comes of his dreams."

31 Then they got Joseph's robe, slaughtered a goat and dipped the robe in the blood. 32 They took the ornamented robe back to their father and said, "We found this. Examine it to see whether it is your son's robe."

33 He recognized it and said, "It is my son's robe! Some ferocious animal has devoured him. Joseph has surely been torn to pieces."

34 Then Jacob tore his clothes, put on sackcloth and mourned for his son many days. 35 All his sons and daughters came to comfort him, but he refused to be comforted. "No," he said, "in mourning will I go down to the grave [c] to my son." So his father wept for him.

36 Meanwhile, the Midianites [d] sold Joseph in Egypt to Potiphar, one of Pharaoh's officials, the captain of the guard.

Genesis 43

3 Then ten of Joseph's brothers went down to buy grain from Egypt. 6 Now Joseph was the governor of the land, the one who sold grain to all its people. So when Joseph's brothers arrived, they bowed down to him with their faces to the ground. 7 As soon as Joseph saw his brothers, he recognized them, but he pretended to be a stranger and spoke harshly to them. "Where do you come from?" he asked.

"From the land of Canaan," they replied, "to buy food."

8 Although Joseph recognized his brothers, they did not recognize him.

1 Then Joseph could no longer control himself before all his attendants, and he cried out, "Have everyone leave my presence!" So there was no one with Joseph when he made himself known to his brothers. 2 And he wept so loudly that the Egyptians heard him, and Pharaoh's household heard about it.

4 Then Joseph said to his brothers, "Come close to me." When they had done so, he said, "I am your brother Joseph, the one you sold into Egypt! 5 And now, do not be distressed and do not be angry with yourselves for selling me here, because it was to save lives that God sent me ahead of you. 6 For two years now there has been famine in the land, and for the next five years there will not be plowing and reaping. 7 But God sent me ahead of you to preserve for you a remnant on earth and to save your lives by a great deliverance.

8 "So then, it was not you who sent me here, but God. He made me father to Pharaoh, lord of his entire household and ruler of all Egypt. 9 Now hurry back to my father and say to him, 'This is what your son Joseph says: God has made me lord of all Egypt. Come down to me; don't delay. 10 You shall live in the region of Goshen and be near me—you, your children and grandchildren, your flocks and herds, and all you have. 11 I will provide for you there, because five years of famine are still to come. Otherwise you and your household and all who belong to you will become destitute.'

14 Then he threw his arms around his brother Benjamin and wept, and Benjamin embraced him, weeping. 15 And he kissed all his brothers and wept over them. Afterward his brothers talked with him.

25 So they went up out of Egypt and came to their father Jacob in the land of Canaan. 26 They told him, "Joseph is still alive! In fact, he is ruler of all Egypt." Jacob was stunned; he did not believe them. 27 But when they told him everything Joseph had said to them, and when he saw the carts Joseph had sent to carry him back, the spirit of their father Jacob revived. 28 And Israel said, "I'm convinced! My son Joseph is still alive. I will go and see him before I die."

Lesson (Teacher Words In Bold): Joseph & How God Can Make Good Out Of Bad

Hold a lemon up before the students. The lemon should be wrapped in several layers of plastic wrap, which can be tied off with a twist tie or rubber band at the bottom for security.

How many of you have heard of the expression, "When given a lemon, make lemonade?" Yes.

What does the expression mean? Variations of when something bad happens, make something good out of it.

How did Joseph "make lemons out of lemonade" after his brothers sold him into slavery? He worked hard as a slave; he was rewarded by being given powerful positions and his freedom. He was able to save a lot of people from starving.

Think of a time you got sick. Sickness can be terrible and not much fun. Think of good things that happened because of it. (Example: Some child was hospitalized, but he got lots of toys and gifts, got to miss school, and he learned courage facing shots and needles).

While you're thinking, we're going to play pass the lemon. Tell the group about the time you got sick. First tell some of the worst things about that sickness. If you can think of something good that happened because of it, you get to put your initials on the plastic wrap around lemon with this pen. Then, you'll pass it to the next person.

As the lemon is passed and signed, discuss these things. If a child thinks of something bad that happened, try to help him or her think of something good that came of it, even if it was just being a stronger person.

Put the lemon aside for the moment.

Let's really make lemonade out of lemons.

Bring out a bunch of lemons cut up, and let the students squeeze the juice into a cup.

Let's pretend this sour lemon juice is our bad feelings about that sickness. We are going to squeeze the bad feelings in with the sugar and water. After that, we'll remember better the good things that came from it.

If there is not enough juice to make a cup, supplement with bottled lemon juice. Add a cup of sugar and eight cups of water. Stir. Pour into cups and let the students enjoy.

Let's pass our special lemon again while we're drinking. This time, let's talk about families. Joseph's brothers thought they were doing a terrible thing to him, didn't they? Yes.

And it was terrible! How would you feel if your brother or sister sold you away from your parents? Think of the worst argument you have ever had with a sister or brother. As we pass the lemon, the person holding it can tell us what happened in that argument.

Let students tell and use trigger questions:

Who started it? Did you do anything mean back? How would you have handled it differently if you had it to do over again?

As each child finishes telling, have him sign the initials of his brother or sister on the lemon, beside where he signed his own.

After all have finished:

We know that Jesus wants brothers and sisters to get along. Just like Joseph forgave his brothers, we need to forgive our family. They're the only family we have and we should appreciate them. We know that Jesus forgives a bad fight with a sister or brother. He washes away our past wrongs...

Take the cellophane off the lemon and throw it in the trash.

And makes it like we're new again! When we go home today, let's try to treat our brothers and sisters like those fights never happened. Let's follow Joseph's example.

Intro Activity, Younger Children: Draw Your Family

Give each child a sheet of construction paper and tell them to draw a picture of their family. Tell them to be prepared to say what a nice thing about each person they draw.

Intro Activity, Older Children:
Describing Your Family

Give each child a sheet of paper with three lines drawn to create four columns. Tell them to make a column for three people in their family. Tell them to try to think of ten words—good or bad—to describe each person.

Activity, Younger Children:
Working Together

Divide the class into pairs. If there are an odd number of children, make one group of three. Using old neckties or pieces of string, tie the two children's wrists together, left to right. Have them put their free hands behind their back and tell them they can only use the hands that are tied together.

It's important in life to work together. Sometimes it's hard. We don't always want to do things the same way as somebody else. We are not always as coordinated as the next person. We have to have patience when people do things slower or faster or more easily than we do.

In Joseph's family, nobody wanted to work together with Joseph. They thought he was young and stupid, and they were jealous.

Let's see how well we can work with the person we're tied to and see if we can't do better.

Have them perform the following tasks:

- Rearranging the toys on the toy shelf.
- Picking all the orange crayons out of the crayon basket and putting them aside.
- Putting three animal crackers on each napkin for students during snack.
- Wiping off the book shelves with a wet paper towel.

If they run into difficulties, ask them, **What can we do so you can work well together?** Offer suggestions like taking turns using their tied hands, one working and the other relaxing, and then switching.

Have them switch jobs. At the end, untie all wrists and have them take a seat.

How many of you worked well together?

How many had a problem at first and didn't work well together?

What did you do to solve the problem?

When you go home today, if you have a problem with your sister or brother, will you try to work with them?

Generate discussion on some of the challenges they have with siblings and some solutions to keep arguments from starting.

Activity, Older Children: Role Play: Getting Along with Siblings

Write the following skills on a board or sheets of paper posted to the wall (you can skip the examples and merely give them verbally). Have each child pick one of the following scenarios out of a hat. She should read the scenario and then read the response by the sibling. It will not be the best way to respond, but it will be typical. Have the children use the skills to prevent envy, bitterness or poor communication skills from starting a heated argument.

Example: Lindsay watched her mom and sister Jessica return from shopping. There was a bunch of new stuff for Lindsay and only one thing for Jessica.

Lindsay's response: Not fair! You *always* favor her! As if I don't need stuff too! If you don't want me in this family, just say so!!

Skill #1: Speak plainly, clearly and honestly without raising your voice. (i.e. "When you take Jessica shopping and leave me home, I really get my feelings hurt. I wonder why you didn't think to get me even a pair of socks.")

Skill #2 Say something positive before airing your complaint. (i.e. "I'm really happy for Jessica that she got all these new clothes, but I feel left out. I need things too.")

Skill #3: Repeat what the other person says so that they feel confident you are listening and not just asking to be heard. (i.e. "I know that you have a party this weekend and wanted something new to wear, but I've made do with the same old clothes for the last six months.")

Skill #4: Don't generalize. Phrases like, "You *never* think about me." "It's *always* all about my sister," cannot possibly be true, so saying them discredits your argument. Try for facts: "The last two times you went shopping, you went with Jess and left me home."

Skill #5: Use "I feel" statements rather than accusations. "I feel ignored sometimes."

Scenarios

1. Jon's brother, who is two years younger, has Jon's same bedtime. When Jon was Andrew's age, he had to go to bed a whole hour earlier.
   Jon's response: He gets away with murder! You don't treat us fairly! If he's allowed to stay up until nine, then I should be able to stay up until ten!

2. Jen's big sister Kaleigh got braces two years ago. Jen's teeth are actually more crooked than Kaleigh's were and she is so self-conscious she's afraid to smile sometimes. However, her parents have told Jen they cannot afford to get her braces until Kaleigh is done. It will be another two years! Jen will be a freshman in high school and still wearing braces.
   Jen's response: How is that fair? She gets to look great and I have to start high school looking like a dork? She always gets everything, and you guys are just not fair to me!

3. Tyler gets straight A's on almost every report card. His younger brother gets B's and C's. His parents often tell Alex, "You're just too smart for school. You're bored, is all. When you're older, people will see your genius shine through." Mom and Dad used to award money for A's and B's, but once they realized Tyler was always getting more money, they changed it so that Tyler got a dollar for an A, but Alex got two dollars for an A.
   Tyler's response at the next report card: You're always telling Alex how wonderful he is! The fact is, if he would sit there and do the work like I do, he'd get good grades, too! He's getting two dollars for being lazy, whereas I'm getting a dollar for working hard! You just always favor him!

4. Mary Kate's big sister Alyssa is tall, lean and has beautiful chestnut hair. She's always being invited to a party or has friends over. Mary Kate is short and has the type of looks that people just seem to see through. She's quieter but probably more thoughtful. Alyssa had a huge birthday party this year, and Mary Kate overheard her parents say that thank God they didn't have to spend the money twice—again for Mary Kate's birthday. She heard her dad say, "She only has two friends. I could take them all to dinner and the movies and it would cost one-tenth the money."
   Mary Kate's response: It's not my fault if Alyssa has more friends. They don't talk about

anything! They're really shallow and all about boys and clothes... If you guys feel like rewarding that, I guess it's none of my business. But I think you should take me and Elaina and Audrey to New York to see a show, at least! You're just as shallow as she is!

5. Ryan's brother Michael is a high school football star. Michael doesn't play a sport, so he really notices how every dinner table conversation is between is dad and brother is all about football. It's as if Michael isn't even there. Sometimes his mom will interrupt loudly to say, "How was *your* day Michael?" But last night, Dad merely looked through him, didn't wait for him to answer, and went back to talking to Michael about football.
   Ryan's response: Hel-lo! Am I the invisible boy? I get so sick of hearing about football at this table that I want to puke. I will never go to a football game again, and I think you all are crazy. Oh, and Mom? You don't have to feel sorry for me. I don't need a family. I've got plenty of friends I can talk to about things that are actually interesting.

Game, Younger Children: Leg Races

Tell every child to pick a partner. Tie the two inside legs of each pair together.

First we learned to work together with our hands. Now we're going to work together with our feet. Let's see if we can cooperate to get things done. We're going to go to the Land of Egypt where Joseph was taken, and then we're going to come back. Let's see if we can work together on our journey better than Joseph's brothers worked with Joseph.

Have them walk down the corridor tied together.

Have them stop at the water fountain to get drinks. **Wow, it's really thirsty out here on our journey to Egypt. Let's work together to get our water without knocking each other over or arguing.**

Have them sit down against the wall to rest. **Wow, it's really tiresome, getting to and from Egypt. Let's sit down to rest without knocking each other over.**

Let's see if we can fan each other to get some of this heat off without knocking each other in the face.

Have them go back to the classroom or outside to a grassy place. Have a two-legged relay race.

This wasn't easy. But Joseph learned to work with whatever circumstances he found himself in. We should be able to also. That's the way to find God's will and end up in the best place possible—tired but victorious like Joseph!

Game, Older Children: Power Racing with Toilet Paper

We've been talking about our siblings and how they and our friends are sometimes hard to get along with. However, if we learn to work together instead of arguing, God can bless us better.

So this is a game of working together.
Have students form pairs. Each pair gets one square of toilet paper. Each party should pinch their lips on opposite sides of the square. Explain that without dropping it or ripping it, they must race to the other end of the room and back.

See what you can figure out about your partner's height, coordination, ability level and try to combine your own with those things.
Start the race.

If they tear the sheet or if one of them drops it from their lips, they have to start over again. The team who gets back first wins.

If you have enough children, this works great as a relay.

Closing Prayer

Dear Lord, Help us to remember this week that families are one of the most important gifts that You have given us. Help us to get along with our sisters and brothers and moms and dads and to forgive them when they annoy us. Help us to make lemonade out of any lemons that come our way in the next week. Helps us remember that if Joseph could forgive his brothers, surely we can forgive ours. Help us to remember that.

Amen.

MOSES IS BORN

Children believe that God will help them in times of trouble, but we need to put that theory into action with them.

The lesson of Moses' birth shows how he escaped death when that looked nearly impossible for male Hebrew babies. **God rewards courage that is combined with trust in him**, and Moses' mother had that courage. She put Moses in a basket and let him float out over the waters so he wouldn't be killed by the Egyptians.

We want kids to feel confident that **God helps us find courage in times of trouble**. He loves a faithful heart and is joyful in rewarding it.

MATERIALS LIST

Lesson

- Monster bag head covering
- Snack prizes such as marshmallows, small candies, cookies

Intro Activity for Younger Children

- Large brown shopping bag
- Marker Pens
- Paper Scraps
- Stick glue

Intro Activity for Older Children

- Large brown shopping bag
- Paper plates (cut in half)
- String
- Marker Pens
- Paper Scraps

- Stick glue

Activity, Younger Children

- Blue construction paper, one sheet for each student
- Green construction paper cut into strips: 11.5 x 2.5 inches, one strip for each student
- Two cotton balls for each student
- Brown construction paper, cut into half circles, about 4" wide at the radius
- Glue Sticks
- Scissors

Activity, Older Children

- White construction paper, one sheet for each child. Using a ruler and pen, divide each sheet in half width wise. Then divide the top part in half. Divide the bottom part in thirds. You should now have five boxes on the sheet. Repeat for each child.
- Colored pencils and thin markers

Game, Younger Children

- Snack prizes such as marshmallows, small candies, cookies

Game, Older Children

- Paper plates (cut in half so one plate is needed per two students),
- Markers
- Colored paper scraps
- A hat or bag to put the questions in

Exodus 1-2

6 Now Joseph and all his brothers and all that generation died, 7 but the Israelites were fruitful and multiplied greatly and became exceedingly numerous, so that the land was filled with them.

8 Then a new king, who did not know about Joseph, came to power in Egypt. 9 "Look," he said to his people, "the Israelites have become much too numerous for us. 10 Come, we must deal shrewdly with them or they will become even more numerous and, if war breaks out, will join our enemies, fight against us and leave the country."

11 So they put slave masters over them to oppress them with forced labor, and they built Pithom and Rameses as store cities for Pharaoh. 12 But the more they were oppressed, the more they multiplied and spread; so the Egyptians came to dread the Israelites 13 and worked them ruthlessly. 14 They made their lives bitter with hard labor in brick and mortar and with all kinds of work in the fields; in all their hard labor the Egyptians used them ruthlessly.

15 The king of Egypt said to the Hebrew midwives, whose names were Shiphrah and Puah, 16 "When you help the Hebrew women in childbirth and observe them on the delivery stool, if it is a boy, kill him; but if it is a girl, let her live." 17 The midwives, however, feared God and did not do what the king of Egypt had told them to do; they let the boys live. 18 Then the king of Egypt summoned the midwives and asked them, "Why have you done this? Why have you let the boys live?"

19 The midwives answered Pharaoh, "Hebrew women are not like Egyptian women; they are vigorous and give birth before the midwives arrive."

20 So God was kind to the midwives and the people increased and became even more numerous. 21 And because the midwives feared God, he gave them families of their own.

22 Then Pharaoh gave this order to all his people: "Every boy that is born [b] you must throw into the Nile, but let every girl live."

Exodus 2: The Birth of Moses

1 Now a man of the house of Levi married a Levite woman, 2 and she became pregnant and gave birth to a son. When she saw that he was a fine child, she hid him for three months. 3 But when she could hide him no longer, she got a papyrus basket for him and coated it with tar

and pitch. Then she placed the child in it and put it among the reeds along the bank of the Nile. 4 His sister stood at a distance to see what would happen to him.

5 Then Pharaoh's daughter went down to the Nile to bathe, and her attendants were walking along the river bank. She saw the basket among the reeds and sent her slave girl to get it. 6 She opened it and saw the baby. He was crying, and she felt sorry for him. "This is one of the Hebrew babies," she said.

7 Then his sister asked Pharaoh's daughter, "Shall I go and get one of the Hebrew women to nurse the baby for you?"

8 "Yes, go," she answered. And the girl went and got the baby's mother. 9 Pharaoh's daughter said to her, "Take this baby and nurse him for me, and I will pay you." So the woman took the baby and nursed him. 10 When the child grew older, she took him to Pharaoh's daughter and he became her son. She named him Moses, [a] saying, "I drew him out of the water."

Lesson (Teacher Words in Bold): Moses' Birth- His Mother Takes Action

We're going to play a game that puts us in Moses' mother's shoes. She had a scary choice. If she did *nothing*, her son Moses would be killed by bad men. If she did *something*, it was risky and he still might die, but *something* was better than *nothing*.

If we step out in faith and do *something*, even if we're not really smart or really big or really strong, we can count on the fact that God protects people who show courage.

Let's play the Monster Game and pretend we are as courageous as Moses' mother.

Have all children except one huddle in a corner. Have the one excluded child be the monster. The monster will wear a scary bag over his head so he can't see. Have him stand in the center of the room facing the corner where the children are huddled.

Each time the teacher says, **"Monster, advance!"** the monster should take one giant step forward. After the second time she says **"Monster, advance!"** the children are free to try to leave the corner for their destination, which is "The Water," the other corner. The monster should reach out when he hears or senses someone moving and try to tag people. If children are tagged, they are captives of the giant and must sit off to the side. If they get past him, they should make it to the safety of "The Water."

Allow several children to be the monster. Then bring them all back together for a discussion.

What would have happened to you if you had stayed in the corner? They would surely have gotten tagged.

What would have happened to Moses if his mother had stayed in her corner, meaning she did nothing to get her baby away from the Egyptians? Moses would have been killed.

What is a "risk?" What does it mean to "take a risk?" It means you do something rather than nothing.

Most (all) of you risked leaving the corner to keep the monster from catching you. The game prize doesn't just go to the people who reached "The Water," or who "got there first." The prize goes to...

...anyone who left the corner. (Give out prizes to all: a few M&MS, marshmallows, cookies, etc.)

Why is that? Why am I rewarding all those who left the corner? Because they all showed courage and they all took a risk.

- **Moses' mother was not a genius. A baby could have drowned in that water.**
- **She was not a strong warrior. She had a baby only three months ago.**
- **She was not rich. She was a slave.**
- **She was not perfect.**
- **She had a mother's love, and when it came time to show courage, she didn't just stand there, too afraid to do anything. She trusted that God would help her.**
- **God rewarded Moses' mother's love and her courage.**

If you show courage to do the right thing, God will help you too.

Intro Activity, Younger Children: Making The Monster Mask

Put a big brown bag in the center of the art table with the shoulders cut out so that it comes down to the chest. *Do not cut out the eyes.* Put out marker pens and paper scraps that might be used for hair. If the children are young, draw on the scary eyes yourself.

Today, we're going to play the MONSTER GAME. So right now we are making a scary monster mask. Everyone add what you want to the bag, so it looks scary.

Intro Activity, Older Children:
Making The Monster Mask

Cut paper plates in half and punch two holes so that students can tie a piece of string or yarn and make a mask. Have each student decorate his/her mask with marker pens, paper scraps, or any other materials.

Alternatively, the teacher can use the big brown bag in the center of the art table with the shoulders cut out so that it comes down to the chest. *Do not cut out the eyes.* Put out marker pens and paper scraps that might be used for hair. If the children are young, draw on the scary eyes yourself.

Today, we're going to play the MONSTER GAME. So right now we are making a monster mask. Everyone add what you want to the bag or paper plate, so it looks scary.

Activity, Younger Children:
Baby Moses in the Reeds

Give each child the items on the supplies list.

They each should:

1. Make deep cuts into the green strip, maybe four per inch, so that the standing pieces look like blades of grass (reeds).
2. Paste or glue the strip across the bottom of the blue construction paper.
3. Paste the two cotton balls together behind the reeds so that part of the cotton cluster is sticking up.
4. Draw lines on the brown half-circle of construction paper, so that it looks like a basket.
5. Paste the basket around the cotton balls and under it so that the cotton balls stick out the top.
6. Draw on the sun, some flowers, and the words MOSES GOT AWAY!

Activity, Older Children:
Moses' Mom's Courage

Have children take turns reading the following scenarios and trying to say what they would do in each example. As answers arise, the group can discuss them. Use these questions and add to them if you wish:

1. You're on a school bus. The kids in the back are shouting mean things to a quieter kid who has few or no friends. What would you do? How might you show courage?
2. There's a girl in your class who never does her homework, especially in math. On the day of the math test, she sits beside you, and you feel her looking on your paper every minute or so, copying your answers. What would you do? How might you show courage?
3. Your mom has told you many times that if you don't confront certain people, they won't respect you. There's a bully on the playground who keeps calling you names. You're afraid if you confront him, it will cause him to start a fight, and you don't want that either. How do you handle him?
4. A girl in your class is handing out party invitations. She invites some girls and skips others, not seeming to care who sees or gets hurt. Your best friend doesn't get an invitation. What would you do? How might you show courage?
5. Your two best friends get in a fight and have been giving each other the silent treatment for two days. You've been doing your best to not get involved. Finally one of them says to you, "Choose. You can be friends with me or her." What do you do?
6. A girl on your street gets cancer, is in and out of the hospital, and has lost all of her hair. She can't go to school and is lonely. Your mom wants you to spend some time every week with her, because that's what she would want other kids to do if you got that sick. But being around her scares you…she wasn't exactly a good friend, and it's kind of a grim reminder that bad things can happen, and you don't know when or to whom. What do you do?
7. A kid in school confides in you that his dad drinks and gets violent, hitting him and his mother and breaking things around the house. He makes you swear not to tell anyone. What do you do?
8. You recently saw a car accident while driving in your family's car and it was pretty horrible. In school you hear your friend bragging that his big brother takes their parents' car at night and drives a hundred miles an hour down this back road that doesn't see a whole lot of traffic. Do you keep the story to yourself? What do you do?

Game, Younger Children:
Monster at the Door

Line the children up on the opposite wall of the room as the door. Have an assistant or someone willing to help stand on the outside so the children can't see who it is. Have everyone join hands.

When I was a little girl, I was afraid of monsters. I was afraid one would knock on my door like this:

Knock on the wall: KNOCK-KNOCK, knock-knock. KNOCK-KNOCK, knock-knock.

I was afraid he would come into my room and have long, gross fingernails, and he would scratch me and try to bite me.

The assistant should do the monster knock at the door: KNOCK-KNOCK, knock-knock. KNOCK-KNOCK, knock-knock. Pretend you're really scared.

I don't want to go anywhere near that door! But I'm going to take one step forward with courage. Will you take one step with me?

The assistant should do the monster knock at the door: KNOCK-KNOCK, knock-knock. KNOCK-KNOCK, knock-knock.

Do you think it's a monster? Some will say yes; some will say no.

But what if it is the monster? Only one way to find out! Let's take another step of courage.

The assistant should do the monster knock at the door: KNOCK-KNOCK, knock-knock. KNOCK-KNOCK, knock-knock.

What if he's huge and massive and ugly? What if he tries to bite me in the head? Let's take another step of courage.

The assistant should do the monster knock at the door VERY LOUDLY: KNOCK-KNOCK, knock-knock. KNOCK-KNOCK, knock-knock.

It's better to move forward with courage than to do nothing. We learned that from Moses' mother. Let's all take another step.

Ferocious knocking by this point from assistant.

Sometimes we get so afraid of things that we can't remember what's real and what isn't. It takes courage to figure out what's real.

Open the door. The assistant should be standing there, smiling and holding a plate of treats.

Sometimes, if we move forward with courage to conquer our fears, we find that God has a really nice surprise in mind for us instead of something scary!

Open the door and have the assistant pass out marshmallow, cookie or candy treats.

Game, Older Children: Cartoon Designs

Take the pieces of white paper with the lines drawn in them and distribute one to each child. Give them colored pencils.

Pretend you're a cartoonist. You have five sequences—five boxes in which to tell a story. Take the question you answered in the Moses' Mom's Courage game. Draw a cartoon of yourself in that situation. Don't forget to draw in conversation bubbles!

Closing Prayer

Father in heaven, Thank you for the example of Moses' mother and how her courage gave us one of the greatest leaders of all time. Help us to show courage this week when we're trying to do the right thing and to remember that You love to reward those who step forward.

Amen.

Made in the USA
Monee, IL
01 March 2021

61685607R00031